SELF-PO

PATRICK KAVANAGH

Self-Portrait

PHOTOGRAPHS BY LIAM MILLER

THE DOLMEN PRESS

Set in Baskerville type and printed
and published in the Republic of Ireland
at the Dolmen Press,
North Richmond Industrial Estate,
North Richmond Street,
Dublin 1

First published 1964
Second edition, reset, 1975

ISBN 0 85105 275 4

Distributed in the U.S.A. and in Canada
by Humanities Press Inc.,
171 First Avenue, Atlantic Highlands, N. J. 07716

PREFACE TO A PREFACE

This is not a completely true self-portrait,
and its lack of truth is not due to its short-
ness. For years I have tried to find a technique through which a man might reveal

5

himself without embarrassment. There are two fairly successful examples of this technique — *Don Quixote* and Joyce's *Ulysses.* Sancho Panza and Mr. Bloom are the private lives of two public men. I have found that only in verse can one confess with dignity. We have all done mean and ugly things and nearly always these sins should be confessed because of the damage they have done us. Even the most apparently revealing autobiographies (some like Pepys' *Diaries* in code) do not expose too much.

My life has been a failure till I woke this morning, which is the 24th August, 1963. I saw a wonder question mark:

> *There is to-day*
> *And tomorrow.*

I echoed Carlyle:

> *So here hath been dawning*
> *Another blue day,*
> *Think wilt thou let it*
> *Slip useless away.*

Probably yes. But continuation is everything.

Patrick Kavanagh

SELF-PORTRAIT

I DISLIKE TALKING ABOUT MY-SELF in a direct way. The self is only interesting as an illustration. For some reason, whenever we talk about our personal lives they turn out to be both irrelevant and untrue — even when the facts are right, the mood is wrong.

English publishers and newspapers are mad for personal data, especially about people from Ireland. They love Irishmen. America is now even worse. And the unfortunate peoples of my island home lap up all that vulgarity when it is dished out to them.

The quality that most simple people fear — and by simple people I mean terrified, ignorant people — is the comic spirit, for the comic spirit is the ultimate sophistication which they do not understand and therefore fear.

When, under the evil ægis of the so-called Irish Literary Movement, I wrote a dreadful stage-Irish, so-called autobiography called *The Green Fool*, the common people of this country gobbled up this stage-Irish lie. When, years later, I wrote *Tarry Flynn* which I am humble enough to claim is not only the best but the only *authentic* account of life as it was lived in Ireland this century (a man shouldn't be afraid to tell the truth even when it is in favour of himself), the principal people who enjoyed this novel were literary sophisticates; its uproarious comedy was too much for the uneducated reader. I am not trying to boost my wares. I am merely trying to illustrate a position. And I would say now that that so-called Irish Literary Movement which purported to be frightfully Irish and racy of the Celtic soil was a thoroughgoing English-bred lie. Anybody can write tragedy. The English reviewers went crazy about the poetry of O'Casey's *Juno*, whereas in fact we only endure that embarrassment for the laughs in Captain Boyle.

I am supposed to be self-portraying myself and I hope I am so doing. I can tell all about my background and upbringing without being very original. And it is there the lie comes in. I would have to show that my background and my childhood adventures were out of the common just as journalists do when they report on foreign countries. I remember reading a journalist on a visit to Greece who made the illuminating disclosure that the Greeks were very fond of conversation. But if the place and the experience weren't different what the devil was he doing out there?

My childhood experience was the usual barbaric life of the Irish country poor. I have never seen poverty properly analysed. Poverty is a mental condition. You hear of men and women who have chosen poverty, but you cannot choose poverty. Poverty has nothing to do with eating your fill today; it is anxiety about what's going to happen next week. The cliché poverty that you get in the working-class novel or play is a formula.

My father, being a shoemaker, was probably less poor than the small farmer classes. What was called the 'dropping shilling' kept coming in. But as for the *scraidíns* of farmers with their watery little hills that would physic a snipe, I don't know where they got any money. But the real poverty was the lack of enlightenment to get out and get under the moon.

I am afraid this fog of unknowing affected me dreadfully. But, as I have suggested earlier, all this is of little importance.

Whatever tradition of semi-civilised living existed in Carleton's time, it was not there in mine. I fell between two stools.

Round about the late nineteen-thirties a certain prosperity came through and foolishly enough that was the time I chose to leave my native fields. I had no messianic impulse to leave. I was happy. I went against my will. A lot of our actions are like that. We miss the big emotional gesture and drift away. Is it possible to achieve our potential grand passion? I believe so. Perhaps that has been my weakness.

I CAME TO DUBLIN in nineteen-thirty-nine. It was the worst mistake of my life. The Hitler war had started. I had my comfortable little holding of watery hills beside the Border. What was to bate it for a life? And yet I wasted what could have been my four glorious years begging and scrambling around the streets of malignant Dublin. I could have done my smuggling stint. I could never see my own interest. I could never see love on bended knees begging me to come. I was always in the fog.

When I came to Dublin in 1939 the Irish Literary affair was still booming. It was the notion that Dublin was a literary metropolis and Ireland, as invented and patented by Yeats, Lady Gregory and Synge, a spiritual entity. It was full of writers and poets and I am afraid I thought their work had the Irish quality. The conversation in Poets' Pub had the richness and copiosity that H. W. Nevinson said all Dublin conversation had. To me, even then, it was tiresome drivel between journalists and civil servants. No humour at all. And, of course, they thought so much of poetry they didn't believe in the poet ating. I am not, I assure you, complaining, merely stating a few ridiculous facts. It was all my fault.

What was I doing there? Wasn't I old enough to know the differ? Shouldn't I have cottoned on? Ah well, we live and we sometimes learn.

Now, part of my poverty-stricken upbringing was my belief in respectability — a steady job, decency. The bohemian rascals living it up in basements and in mountain hideouts horrified me. If I had joined them and endured them they'd have taken me to their bosoms. But I couldn't do it. Instinctively I realised that they were embittered people worshipping the poor man's poet. Their left-wingery was defeat. But the key to prosperity was with that sort of enemy and still is. When I think of the indignities I endured in the cause of respectability I can kick myself. And me with health and strength to dig ditches, or to leap them anyway with a sack of white flour on me back. The Monaghan-Armagh-Louth border was not a severe test for a true stayer carrying top weight. I can kick myself for all the people I didn't kick then. Sometimes when walking along a Dublin street I might well be noticed making wild, vicious kicks at emptiness and scringing my teeth at the same time. Thinking over the matter in the light of hindsight,

I realise it would not have been easy for a man of sensibility to survive in the society of my birth, but it could have been done had I been trained in the technique of reserve and restraint. A poet is never one of the people. He is detached, remote, and the life of small-time dances and talk about football would not be for him. He might take part but could not belong.

A poet has to have an audience — half a dozen or so. Landor, who said he esteemed ten a sufficient audience, was very optimistic. I know about half a dozen and these are mainly London-based. It may be possible to live in total isolation but I don't understand how. The audience is as important as the poet. There is no audience in Ireland, though I have managed to build up out of my need a little audience for myself. The real problem is the scarcity of a right audience which draws out of a poet what is best in him. The Irish audience that I came into contact with tried to draw out of me everything that was loud, journalistic and untrue. Such as:

> *My soul was an old horse*
> *Offered for sale in twenty fairs.*

Anthologists everywhere keep asking for

this. Also asked for is another dreadful job about Mother Ireland:

> *It would never be summer*
>   *always autumn*
> *After a harvest always lost.*

Thank God, I control the copyrights in these poems and nobody can use them. What the alleged poetry-lover loved was the Irishness of a thing. Irishness is a form of anti-art. A way of posing as a poet without actually being one. The New Lines poets of today have invented a similar system.

They are also sympathetic to the Irish thing.

No young person today would think of coming to live in Dublin as a metropolis. A new awareness is in the air. A couple of years ago I remember a young chap accosting me in a Dublin street. He was from the southern part of Eire and he was on his way to Rome — to take up the poetry trade. He was right too. At least something might happen to him there, a rich woman might take a fancy to his poetry and keep him in the decency and comfort which are a necessity of the poet. I pause here to emphasise that I have no belief in the virtue of a place. Many misguided persons imagine that living in France or Italy is the equivalent of a liberal education. French in particular is the language of art. Still, Dublin hasn't the possibilities for getting hitched up to a rich woman, and this is about the only way a true poet can remain true and keep up an adequate supply of good whiskey.

AND NOW IT'S AROUND 1955 and I am wandering around Dublin when I run into a poetry-lover.

'How are you getting on at all?' says he with much pity.

The instinct to do a day's good deed has always been a weakness with me, so I reply, 'Terrible'.

'Poor fella.'

'Sure what can I do?'

'And you're not writing any poetry these times. I never see anything by you in the *Irish Times*. The flash is gone. I say, the flash is gone.'

'I suppose so.'

'A terrible scandal that the Government doesn't do something for our Irish poets. There's forty or fifty major poets in this country today and if I had me way they'd all have a civil list pension. Peadar has been working for that this many a year. Is the health all right again?'

I cough hard and send him away happy. I won't be long in it and that City Hall booking for my lying-in-state can be taken up. And that was interesting too. When I was above in the Rialto Hospital, and the report of my impending demise spread, two well-wishers decided to do me proud in death: they would have me waked in the City Hall. A journalist friend of mine brought me the news as I lay in hospital at the end of a real tether, which was attached to the bottom of the bed and to rise sitting you pulled on the rope. It must have been disappointing that I didn't oblige.

I fear that the mood I have been evoking may give the impression that what happened to me is important and that I am important. Nobody is important. Nobody is major. We get to our destiny in the end. I am not in the least bitter over all this. In fact I am always in danger of bursting out laughing.

I merely state the facts. Of course I do not blame some of these people. I had been assailing the myth of Ireland by which they were managing to beat the artistic rap. I had seen and shewn that this Ireland thing was an undignified business — the trade of enemies and failures.

The English lower orders and their voices, the popular journalists, wanted a certain image of the Irishman, one that would make them feel better, but of recent years a small group of Irishmen in London founded an enclave which did not tolerate such blackguardism. Some of those newspapermen were very humble if they happened to be allowed into that company, and they knew their place better than to write about them. That is indeed one thing to be said for English newspapers, they hardly ever gossip about poets — only actors and film and telly stars. I love reading that stuff, the handouts telling us of the stars and their affairs off the set. All supposed to be real life stuff.

FOR A NUMBER OF YEARS I was a film critic. I attended the Irish Film Society shows of a Saturday and wrote as enthusiastically as the next man about the marvellous Italian film—the photograpy, the direction and the director, a man of superb genius. That was before I learned the difficult art of not caring, of having the courage of one's feelings. But it did take me quite a while before I came out with the terrible disclosure that I thought of most of these foreign films what George the Third thought of Shakespeare — poor stuff, but one mustn't say so.

I burned my way through the film critics' world till in the end I was unable to say another word. If I had been able to stick it out I would probably today be a maker of films or a director of telly shows, or even one of those suave chaps who talk on telly and who are all noted for an excellent head of hair and who all have the same smiling face, the same age too, frozen at 39. See what I missed and see what the public missed. And there's where it was.

Among the other things I missed, one I regret was refusing the offer of Reuters to go in as a reporter with the Second Front. And look at the fellow who wrote *The Longest Day.*

Once again and as always, I was showing my cautious, respectable mentality. Instead of letting it rip. This has been a great defect in my nature. On the other hand I know of quite a couple of very fine poets in England who avoided the draft, one by pretending to be bonkers. But every man to his fancy. I was a different class of animal. I should have done something.

Another great experience I had was my law case, hereinafter to be known as The Trial or Trial and Error, mostly error. Curious thing is that an event so seemingly large at the time disappears in the perspective of a few years. What seems of public importance is never of any importance. Stupid poets and artists think that by taking subjects of public importance it will help their work to survive. There is nothing as dead and damned as an important thing. The things that really matter are casual, insignificant little things, things you would be ashamed to talk of publicly. You are ashamed and then after years someone blabs and you find that you are in the secret majority. Such is fame.

Of my early Dublin experiences I have little of value to offer. In the frosty winter of 1946 I went around trying to sell a contraption for attaching to furnaces to conserve the heat which was scarce those days. I spent a fortnight tramping the frozen streets, my contraption rejected and denounced by all sorts of janitors. Eventually, in the furnace (not the bargain) basement of a Grafton Street store, the boss foreman made a complimentary remark about my article as shown in the illustrated folder. I couldn't carry the machine which was a hundredweight. Twenty-five pounds was the price, but he said there wasn't a whit the matter with the idea if it came at a fiver. 'Worth about a fiver for a trial,' he said. Morality triumphed over commerce. I said, 'It's not worth five shillings never mind five pounds; it's a complete fraud.'

IN THOSE DAYS IN DUBLIN the big thing besides being Irish was peasant quality. They were all trying to be peasants. They had been at it for years but I hadn't heard. And I was installed as the authentic peasant, and what an idea that was among rascals pretending to have an interest in poetry. Although the literal idea of the peasant is of a farm labouring person, in fact a peasant is all that mass of mankind which lives below a certain level of consciousness. They live in the dark cave of the unconscious and they scream when they see the light. They take offence easily, their degree of insultability is very great. I have written:

But I, trained in the slum pubs of Dublin
Among the most offensive class of all
The artisans — am equal to the problem;
I let it ride and there is nothing over.
I understand through all these years
That my difference in their company is an
*   intrusion*

That tears at the sentimental clichés.
They can see my heart squirm when their
*   star rendites*
The topmost twenty in the lowered lights.
No sir, I did not come unprepared.

Which brings me to something that I
might say is the very heart of the matter
of human contentment or as near as we
can get. This is the secret of learning how
not to care. Not caring is really a sense of
values and feeling of confidence. A man
who cares is not the master. And one can
observe this is the matter of simple singing
in the rain or in a pub. The fellows who
around Christmas sing in pubs are not just
chaps enjoying themselves. Enjoying themselves has nothing to do with it. They are
expressing themselves. This is their art,
their reason for existence. And they are
usually very humble and ashamed of their
own selves, for they always assume the part

21

of some singing star or other. No wonder I
squirm. I do not blame them; few people
have the courage to be themselves. And
when they do appear themselves it is all
put on with spade-fulls of bravado. It took
me many years to learn or relearn not to

care. The heart of a song singing it, or a poem writing it, is not caring. I will sing now and give the poems later:

On Raglan Road on an autumn day
I met her first and knew
That her dark hair could weave a snare
that I might one day rue.
I saw the danger yet I walked
upon the enchanted way
And I said let grief be a fallen leaf
at the dawning of the day.

In the beginning of my versing career I had hit on the no-caring jag but there was nobody to tell me that I was on the right track:

My black hills have never seen the sun
rising
Eternally they look north to Armagh.

There are two kinds of simplicity, the simplicity of going away and the simplicity of return. The last is the ultimate in sophistication. In the final simplicity we don't care whether we appear foolish or not. We talk of things that earlier would embarrass. We are satisfied with being ourselves, however small. So it was that on the banks of the Grand Canal between Baggot and

Leeson Street bridges in the warm summer of 1955, I lay and watched the green waters of the canal. I had just come out of hospital. I wrote:

Leafy-with-love banks and the green waters
of the canal
Pouring redemption for me, that I do
The will of God wallow in the habitual, the
banal
Grow with nature again as before I grew.

AND SO IN THIS MOMENT of great daring I became a poet. Except for brief moments in my very early years I had not been a poet. The poems in *A Soul for Sale* are not poetry and neither is *The Great Hunger*. There are some queer and terrible things in *The Great Hunger*, but it lacks the nobility and repose of poetry. The trouble, as I may have mentioned earlier, is that there are so few who would know a poem from a hole in the ground. It is possible on the other hand to recognise a poet, for the animal is recognisable. The main feature about a poet, if you ever happen to meet one — and that's a remote chance, for I can't be everywhere at the one time — the main feature is his humourosity. Any touch

24

of boringness and you are in the wrong
shop. Beautiful women, I am glad to say,
are capable of recognising the baste. Recently a man was presented to me as being
a great poet. He wrote in Irish. I expressed
me doubts and the introducer said: 'How

can you tell when you don't know the language?' That was a sore one, but I was able for it. I said, 'I can't bawl like a cow but I'd know a cow if I saw one.'

That a poet is born, not made, is well known. But this does not mean that he was a poet the day he was physically born. For many a good-looking year I wrought hard at versing but I would say that, as a poet, I was born in or about nineteen-fifty-five, the place of my birth being the banks of the Grand Canal. Thirty years earlier Shancoduff's watery hills could have done the trick but I was too thick to take the hint. Curious this, how I had started off with the right simplicity, indifferent to crude reason and then ploughed my way through complexities and anger, hatred and ill-will towards the faults of man, and came back to where I started. For one of the very earliest things I wrote, even pre-dating Shancoduff, started this way:

> *Child do not go*
> *Into the dark places of soul*
> *For there the grey wolves whine,*
> *The lean grey wolves.*

In that little thing I had become airborne and more; I had achieved weightlessness.

And then I heard about having one's roots
in the soil of being a peasant. And I raged
at Monaghan and the clay and all to that.
But poetry has to do with the reality of the
spirit, of faith and hope and sometimes

even charity. It is a point of view. A poet is a theologian. Arts councils and the like love to believe in the poet as a simple singer piping down the valleys wild. When Shelley said that poets were the real legislators of the world he was right, although he may not have fully understood his rightness. A poet is an original who inspires millions of copies. That's all education consists of — the copying of a good model.

Reverting at that to my public career, I must mention that adventure when I edited and wrote *Kavanagh's Weekly* in 1952. We had no ads. — a distinction that looks like overtaking many other papers before the century is out. I wrote almost the whole paper including the poems, letters to the editor etc. Why do people engage in such madness?

But recently looking up the files I read something that has relevance here. On 'School Book Poetry' I wrote — quoting Longfellow:

There are things of which I may not speak
How strange things happen to a man.
He dabbles in something and does
Not realise that it is his life.

That was what I wrote then. And yet I had

not yet been born, as I believe I afterwards was, though perhaps some folks may not agree. It doesn't matter. Anyhow, I did arrive at complete casualness, at being able to play a true note on a dead slack string.

This year my friend John Jordan, who was about to bring out a magazine called *Poetry Ireland* asked me for a stave and from my redoubt in Monaghan I sent this message to my peoples:

I am here in a garage in Monaghan,
It is a June day and the weather is warm,
Just a little bit cloudy. There's the sun
    again
Lifting to importance my sixteen acre farm.
There are three swallows' nests in the
    rafters above me
And the first clutches are already flying.
Spread this news widely, tell all if you love
    me,
You who knew that when sick I was never
    dying.
(Nae gane, nae gane, nae frae us torn
But taking a rest like John Jordan.)

And so on. One wiseacre said that a garage in Monaghan couldn't be poetry and another of the same mental ilk said that I was going back to me roots and that I was good at that country stuff. Well, there's where it was. Courage is nearly everything. Our pure impulses are always right.

> *In the name of the Father*
> *The Son and the Mother*
> *We explode*
> *Ridiculously, uncode*
> *A habit and find therein*
> *A successful human being.*

Self-Portrait
is the text of a television programme
originally transmitted by
Radio Telefís Eireann
on 30 October 1962

The programme was produced by
Jim FitzGerald